A treatise on Mercersburg theology : or, Mercersburg and modern theology compared

Samuel Miller 1815-1873

A TREATISE

ON

MERCERSBURG THEOLOGY;

OR,

MERCERSBURG AND MODERN THEOLOGY

COMPARED.

BY

SAMUEL MILLER.

PHILADELPHIA:

PUBLISHED BY S. R. FISHER & Co., 54 NORTH SIXTH STREET.

1866.

CONTENTS:

CONTENTS.

PREFACE.

I.

The want of a Church literature of our own, has long since been felt, and become a matter of deep concern. There are good reasons why this feeling should exist in the German Reformed Church, and should make itself heard and understood. It means something more than a desire simply for books written by ministers of our own Church. It is a longing for more, in the various departments of religious literature, of that *better nature and quality,* which can alone be produced by that peculiar mode of thinking, which underlies our distinctive theology. That is what the feeling means and wants, if rightly interpreted.

If we were of the same mind with other surrounding denominations, the case would be different. There would then be little room or occasion for such a feeling. We could conveniently supply ourselves from the abundant store that others have furnished. But we cannot be satisfied with what is thus offered to us; nor remain indifferent to the imperative duty that calls upon us to furnish our people and their children with a different kind of literature. We honestly and sincerely believe the teachings of our own theology, and are convinced that the prevailing religious literature of the day is unsuited to our wants, because of its rationalistic elements, calculated to enervate and undermine a sound religious faith. That is putting the true state of the case in few words.

II.

We here offer an humble contribution to our denominational literature. It is designed, indirectly, to deepen and widen the feeling referred to: to show how truly we stand in need of something better and sounder, than is offered us by most of our modern writers. Those who had fondly hoped that the Church had again settled down to the comfortable conviction, that, after all, there was not much, if any, essential difference between our Mercersburg theology and the prevailing popular theology of the day, were slightly mistaken.

To dispel this notion, if it really existed to any extent, and to bring the subject fresh in review before the mind of the Church, we felt induced to write out a clear, condensed and convincing statement of the manifold and important points of difference between the two systems referred to.

To do this successfully, so as to present the whole in one comprehensive view to the popular mind, and carry conviction at every point, was not an easy task, but required much labor in the way of condensing a great deal that would otherwise have filled a much larger volume, but at the expense of the particular design we had in view. A larger book, or a book encumbered with notes and quotations, would not have answered our purpose to preserve clearly and uninterruptedly the train of thought that connects the various important subjects discussed. If we have succeeded in awakening a desire for more, our object is gained, and that more will yet be abundantly furnished, by other and abler writers.

III.

What of Mercersburg and Modern theology is presented in these pages, is given as it appeared to our mind in the course of our reading and studying for the last twenty years. We hold no one but ourself responsible for what may be peculiar in their subjective apprehension and reproduction. But we are not aware that we have misconstrued or misrepresented the one or the other at a single point. The attempt to fix such a charge on our production, especially in reference to modern theology, when it first appeared in a series of articles in the GERMAN REFORMED MESSENGER, is admitted on all sides to have proved a signal failure.

The point at which our treatise is open to attack, we are told, lies in the use of the term MODERN THEOLOGY; which some suppose to be too general and indefinite, implying more than we intend to express, and is, therefore, liable to misapprehension. It was accordingly suggested to us to define it more explicitly in the sense we use it, to avoid future misunderstandings.

It is true, "Modern Theology," like so many other modern-isms, has not been strictly defined by any previous writer; nor do we think that its friends and admirers would care to have it too strictly defined. It is apt to be stripped of its "glittering generalities," by the glamor of which it has found such general favor. Its strict definition, moreover, involves the principal issue between it and that theology with which it is here contrasted. But as we use the term, for the sake of brevity, rather freely, it may be well enough to explain in the outset more distinctly the sense in which it occurs in our book.

IV.

To relieve the minds of all whom it may concern, we would say, then, in the first place, that those who do not hold, expressly or impliedly, the peculiar views we ascribe to MODERN THEOLOGY, need not allow their equanimity to be disturbed. If they themselves are very clear on this point, then we beg of them to be well assured that we do not mean them or their theology, whatever it may be, or however they may choose to call it. But a great deal of the prevailing and reigning theology of the day, as it meets us in every possible shape and form, does hold and teach, expressly or impliedly, the very things we designate as modern theology. This cannot be denied. It is too well known and understood by every body, to admit of a denial.

But why call it MODERN THEOLOGY? For this reason: because it is, in its distinctive features, a modernism; modern in its origin and conception; in no true sympathy and connection with the ANCIENT faith and teachings of the Church, and an actual DEPARTURE from the confessional and theological position of the Reformation Churches. This is the sense in which we use it. Mercersburg theology, on the contrary, is a deeper and profounder apprehension, and, therefore, VINDICATION of, and not a departure from, the faith and doctrines of the ancient Church and the Reformation. This is the broad distinction between them on this point, as will appear more fully in the treatment of the several subjects, to which the reader's attention is directed in these pages.

With this explanation we commend our book to a careful and thoughtful perusal, in the hope that it may prove a "source of sound instruction and real edification" to all into whose hands it may happen to fall.

INTRODUCTION.

THEOLOGY is a *human* science, treating of divine and supernatural things. It is, therefore, liable to fail in representing a full apprehension of the subject of which it treats, and to embrace views and admit principles, which, when carried out to their logical consequences by merciless critics, are calculated to damage and undermine the very cause of truth, in whose interest and service they are supposed to stand. It is but human to err, and when our theology, as a human science, is found to err, or to be defective, it is our duty to review it, and to reproduce it on more correct principles and a profounder apprehension of its doctrines. How this is to be done, is itself a point of difference, to which we may have occasion to refer.

ROMAN CATHOLIC THEOLOGY passed through this ordeal, and was subjected to a thorough review, the result of which is a deeper and profounder apprehension of the doctrines of Christianity, as reproduced in what is known as Protestant theology, which is accepted by the most enlightened portion of Christendom.

PROTESTANT THEOLOGY, however, was not exempt from the same liability of failing to apprehend fully the system of doctrines, which it exhumed out of the accumulated errors of past ages, or at least to retain it pure and simple; and was subjected, especially in its modern acceptation, to the most unmerciful criticism of German rationalism and infidelity, which induced a theological struggle, such as the world had never witnessed before. It may well be called the life-struggle of theology for the entire Church, fought on the old battle-field of the Sixteenth Century, which resulted for the second time in a triumphant vindication of the truth; but apprehended in a deeper and profounder sense than ever before.

GERMAN EVANGELICAL THEOLOGY, or theology as thus reproduced, and in part still in the act of being reproduced by the ablest and profoundest defenders of our holy Christianity the Church has ever produced, is Protestant still, over against the errors of Rome; but Catholic, at the same time, as embracing the whole truth as underlying the faith of the Church in all ages; and Evangelical, as doing full justice to the positive results of the Reformation. In Germany it is best known by what is called Evangelical Theology, being the product of the united Evangelical Church of that country, Reformed and Lutheran. In this country it is best known as MERCERSBURG THEOLOGY; as the Theological Professors of the Seminary located there, were the first who reproduced it in this country to meet the wants especially of our own MODERN Puritanic and prevailing English and American THEOLOGY. The philosophy which underlies it, is taught in Franklin and Marshall College, transferred from Mercersburg to Lancaster.

MERCERSBURG AND MODERN THEOLOGY COM-
PARED, form an intensely interesting subject.
The difference between them, on almost every
point of doctrine, is so broad and marked, as to
be really startling, and withal of such vast importance as to challenge the serious attention of
all, who are interested in the common cause of
which they treat. Being two broadly distinct
systems throughout, proceeding from two entirely different modes of thinking, it is moreover
impossible to accept both at the same time. We
must either accept the one or the other exclusively, with all the logical consequences it involves. We cannot apply to Mercersburg theology the eclectic mode of accepting a portion of
it and rejecting others. The sooner this is understood by the Reformed Church, in whose
bosom it has found its home, the better it will
be. To be consistent we must either give it up
altogether, as a false and dangerous innovation
throughout, or heartily embrace it as a whole,
as the true sense and meaning of our own theological position as a Church, to the exclusion

entirely of the modern system, of which it is the direct opposite, so far as their distinctive features are concerned. We want more light on this subject, and more generally diffused among ministers and people. The subject has been brought in review before this; but at a time when discussion had excited the feelings and affected, perhaps, to a degree, the impartial and deliberate judgment of those who were interested in the subject. Let us see how Mercersburg and Modern theology compare, when viewed in the absence of all excitement in reference to it. Let us be fair and candid, and try to get at the truth for its own sake, and for the cause in which we are all equally interested. The brief comparison here attempted, makes of course no pretension to completeness, nor to any systematic arrangement, which is not necessary for our purpose, which is simply to present briefly the gist of their various points of difference.

MERCERSBURG AND MODERN THEOLOGY.

CHAPTER I.

§ 1.—ANTHROPOLOGY.

ERCERSBURG theology has rejected as untenable the empiricism of Locke, which still underlies especially our English and American theology, and which denies the existence of innate ideas, and asserts that all our ideas come from sensation and reflection; that is, have their ground and source outside of us. The mind, according to this theory, is constitutionally like a blank sheet of paper, in which there is no self-evolving power to originate an idea or thought, except what is impressed upon it from without, through the medium of our senses, and reproduced into complex forms by the power of reflection. There is, accordingly, no innate basis, grounded in our nature, on which the truth of the existence of things, spiritual and supernatural, can be based, but has to be established by outside evidences alone. Instead of this bald and superficial conception of the constitution of man's nature, the logical consequences of which lead to infidelity, the anthropological premises from which Mercersburg theology proceeds, is the *God-consciousness* in man, which is inherent in our nature, being self-evident, and requiring no proof. The *consciousness of sin* is equally innate and self-evident. The *consciousness of the need of redemption*, as growing out of these, is equally so. These self-evident truths, grounded in the proper self-consciousness of man himself, need not first be established by evidences or arguments derived from other premises, and these again from others, until you are driven back into interminable perplexity and discomfiture by the sharp dialectician, who justly demands self-evident or undeniable premises, from which you attempt to reason. This is one difference between the prevailing modern and Mercersburg theology.* We shall have occasion to speak more particularly of the nature of evidence in its proper connection.

---

§ 2.—THE CENTRAL IDEA.

Another difference is in their central idea. Modern theology makes the atonement or death of Christ, Mercersburg the person of Christ or the incarnation, its central idea. The importance of this difference can be seen in the fact, for instance, that the atonement itself, or justification by faith, cannot be maintained successfully by adopting the former. According to it, the atonement is made to rest primarily on what Christ has done, not on what he is. It apprehends Christ as a mere individual, God and man

---

* See note 1, at the end of the volume, on Dr. B.'s criticism.

in one person, it is true, but yet as a mere individual. Mercersburg theology apprehends Christ as the embodiment of the universal life of humanity, the second Adam or federal head of the race;* and his obedience and death receive their atoning merits from this fact. When he was nailed to the cross, more than a mere individual—humanity itself—was nailed to the cross; consequently whatever merits attach to his suffering and death belong to the race as a whole—not to one individual simply—nor to a limited number of individuals—nor to all individuals numerically considered—but to humanity as a whole (which is something more, and deeper, and broader and more universal, than any number of mere individuals),—subject to appropriation by all who claim them for their individual wants. If Christ had been but a mere individual, one among many, no such universal atonement, nor even a limited atonement, could have been possible. The merits of his death could apply no farther than to himself, and the idea of

---

* See note 2.

the atonement, as available for others, falls to the ground. The idea of one individual dying for the crimes of another individual, does not satisfy the demands of justice. The doctrine of the atonement must be apprehended in a profounder sense than this comes to, and this depends on a proper conception of the person of Christ.

---

§ 3.—THE PERSON OF CHRIST.

The person of Christ, from which the atonement receives all its significance, is thus properly made the central idea in Theology; for not only the atonement, but all other doctrines besides, must be apprehended from this central point of view. As such the doctrine of the person of Christ itself, as already intimated, has received special attention, and is apprehended more profoundly than heretofore. The points of difference between modern and Mercersburg theology, in their Christological conceptions, are numerous and of the utmost importance to the whole system of Christian doctrine.

---

§ 4.—THE INCARNATION.

The incarnation of the Son of God, according to modern theology, implies no more than that he assumed human nature and became an Individual Man. According to Mercersburg theology, he assumed humanity and became the Universal Man, standing related to the race as redeemed in him, as the first Adam stood related to the race as fallen in him. The humanity of the one is as broad, as universal and comprehensive as the humanity of the other. It is in this sense in which the Son of God, when he assumed human nature, became Man, by virtue of its sinless perfection in him, and thereby assumed the whole of its responsibilities to divine justice.

§ 5.—REDEMPTION.

According to modern theology, the Son of God assumed our nature in order that through it, as a means to an end beyond himself, he might procure redemption for humanity as fallen in Adam. According to Mercersburg, the very assumption of that nature, in its sinless perfection, was itself the redemption of humanity. In him humanity stands redeemed already, as the source and fountain of the new race which proceeds from him. In him is our redemption, and by becoming one with him, it is all our own.

----

§ 6.—HYPOSTATICAL UNION.

The hypostatical union, or the union of the divine and human nature in the person of Christ, is real, not only in one person, but in one life, the *divine-human life* of the *God-man*. The terms here used and italicised, and the ideas they convey, are nowhere embodied in modern theology. It has no definite idea what life it is

that is in Christ Jesus, and which is communicated to believers.

---

§ 7.—THE LIFE OF CHRIST.

The life of Christ, communicated to believers,
carries with it, accordingly, his human as well
as his divine nature. Modern theology repu-
diates as obsolete the whole idea, that believers
partake of Christ's humanity.* But in doing so,
it must utterly and hopelessly fail to show, not
only how we can become real partakers of his
divine nature, but how we can become real partakers in the merits of his suffering and death,
which he endured in his human nature. If it
be true, as it tells us, that we have no part in
his human nature, it is bound to show how it
happens that we have part in its merits, or deny
this as well.

---

* See note 3.

§ 8.—IMPUTATION.

Modern theology tries to help itself at this point by means of the doctrine of imputation. The merits of Christ are imputed to believers. But on this same doctrine of imputation, the same wide difference holds between the two systems. According to the modern conception, which views Christ simply as an individual, the imputation of Christ's merits to believers is a mere abstraction, without a corresponding participation of them in fact. According to Mercersburg, the sin of our first parents is imputed to their posterity, because they are involved in it;—and the righteousness of Christ is imputed to believers for the same reason, *i. e.*, because they have part in it by virtue of their union with him.

CHAPTER II.

---

§ 9.—THE ATONEMENT.

TO a sound Christology, there are no difficulties to the Scriptural idea of the atonement, or vicarious sacrifice. The difficulties that present themselves hold only against the abstract modern conception of this doctrine. For instance, when the apostle says, (2 Cor. v. 21,) "Christ was made sin for us, who knew no sin, that we might be made the righteousness of God in him," the question arises, in the first place, how it is reconcilable with divine justice, that Christ, who was without sin, should be accounted and treated as a sinner? and in the second place, how the reverse of this, in our case, is reconcilable with the same divine justice, namely, that

we, who are sinners, should be accounted and
treated as though we had no sin? Both questions demand a solution, in order to vindicate the
doctrine of the atonement. Let us look at the
first, and then at the second of these questions.

It is correct, in a general way, to say, that
both take place by imputation; provided, we do
not apprehend imputation as a mere abstraction,
as is done by modern theology. It is true, the
guilt of our sin was imputed to Christ, as though
he, who knew no sin, were indeed a sinner. But
God ever judges according to truth and justice.
How, then, could the truth and justice of God
hold Christ, who was sinlessly holy, responsible
for the sins of the human race? Not by setting
them simply over to his account, in the abstract
sense in which imputation is generally understood. Here, as elsewhere, imputation must be
apprehended as something more than an abstraction. The imputation of our guilt to Christ, as
in the case of Adam's guilt to his posterity, and
the imputation of Christ's righteousness to believers, is not without a participation of what is

thus imputed.   There must be, and there is, a
perfect justice in accounting Christ responsible
for our sin, though he himself was without sin.
But the truth and justice in the case rest upon
the fact, that he assumed our guilt by assuming
our nature. The assumption of the same human
nature that had sinned, on the part of a sinless
Christ, did not absolve that nature from the
guilt and responsibility of sin.   His assumption
of that nature gave justice the right to hold
him answerable for the guilt of that nature; for
in assuming it, he necessarily assumed all its
debts and liabilities, and, therefore, placed himself under the necessity of rendering satisfaction
for sin.   A man, as far as he himself is concerned, may be free of debts; but by becoming
the proprietor of an estate that is covered with
judgments, for the liabilities of its former owner,
he becomes responsible for these debts the same as
if he had incurred them himself.   By assuming
the proprietorship of the estate, he assumes its
indebtedness, and thereby, and not necessarily
by any debts contracted by himself, he becomes

a debtor to the law, and is justly and legally bound to render satisfaction to its claims. Thus, by assuming our nature that had sinned and is under sentence of condemnation, Christ becomes a debtor to the law, and is, therefore, bound to satisfy the demands of the law, the same as if he himself had incurred the debt. The justice that accounts him responsible does not rest on any sin committed by him, or an abstract assumption of our sins, but on the assumption of our nature that had sinned. Imputation is, therefore, not an abstraction, without reason, truth and justice, but in full accordance with either and all of them. The mere fact that the human nature in the person of Christ is without sin, and perfectly holy, does not exempt it from the guilt and responsibility of sin, as little as our sanctification could justify us before God. As Protestants, we all know that our justification is not effected by our sanctification. As there can be no justification or pardon for the sinner, simply by changing or sanctifying him by the power and operation of the Holy Spirit, so neither could the human nature, that had sinned, be reconciled with God, simply by the fact of Christ's assuming it by the operation of the Holy Ghost, in a state of sinless perfection, *without atoning for its guilt.* On the contrary, by the very assumption of that nature, he became bound to render satisfaction for its guilt, and on the rendering of that satisfaction rests its reconciliation with God. God was in Christ, reconciling the world unto himself, not simply by assuming human nature, but by suffering the penalty of the law in his own person. The assumption of our nature was a free and voluntary act on the part of the Son of God, proceeding from infinite love for a fallen race. The law neither forbade nor demanded his humiliation. But when once freely and voluntarily assumed, then the law demanded, and had a right to demand, full satisfaction for sin. This he rendered by his active and passive obedience, and forms the ground of the sinner's justification before God.

But we now come to the next question, which is precisely the reverse of the one just con-

sidered.   The first is, how a perfectly righteous
man can be justly and truthfully accounted and
treated as a sinner; and the next is, how guilty sinners can justly and truthfully be accounted and
treated as if they were perfectly righteous?   A
successful vindication of the doctrine of the atonement requires also a solution of this question,
bound up and involved as it is in the former; for
"Christ was made sin *for us, that we might be
made the righteousness of God* in him."   The
mere fact that Christ was made sin, who knew
no sin; or, that he assumed the same human nature that had sinned, and thus placed himself under obligation to render satisfaction for sin, does
not yet explain how this is done "*for us;*" how
"*we,*" thereby, *become the righteousness of God.*"
We can understand well enough, from what has
been said, that the satisfaction which he rendered
to the law holds good in reference to human
nature as comprehended in his own person,
whether as individual, or the new federal head
of the race.   But this does not, in itself, en-
lighten us on the question, how we, individually,

are affected by it. The atonement, to be of any
benefit to us, must be vicarious, rendered for us,
and in our stead. The doctrine is, that Christ
died for us, the just for the unjust. How, then,
does it happen that we have part in this objective atonement? How can the truth and justice
of God look upon us sinners as being righteous,
on account of the satisfaction which Christ has
rendered to divine justice?

The learned Bishop Hall replies very perti-
nently to this question by saying: "He is made
our righteousness, as he was made our sin—*imputation doeth both.*" Very good; but imputation here, as in the former case, is clearly not
to be apprehended as a mere abstraction, but
must be in accordance with truth and justice.
Imputation, as a mere abstraction, would fail to
meet the case here as much as it failed in the
other. Christ, who had no sin of his own, was
nevertheless accounted and condemned as though
he were a sinner, and that in full accordance with
truth and justice, BECAUSE HE PARTOOK OF THE
SAME HUMAN NATURE THAT HAD SINNED. On

this the imputation rested. It was this that gave
it truth and justice.   So in the reverse case,
we, who have no righteousness of our own, are
"made the righteousness of God in him," because we partake, by virtue of our union with
him, OF THE SAME HUMAN NATURE THAT KNEW
NO SIN, AND RENDERED SATISFACTION FOR SIN.
On this the imputation in the case rests, and it
is this, and this only, that gives it truth and
justice.   "He was made sin for us, who knew
no sin, that we might be made the righteousness
of God IN HIM."*

---

§ 10.—JUSTIFICATION.

Justification by faith in the merits of Christ,
is, according to modern theology, simply an

---

* This article was penned and inserted here, as its most
appropriate place, after the rest of the series had already
been written and published. It was occasioned by the
reading of a notice of a recent work on the same subject.
It is intended, in its present connection, to show more
fully how utterly powerless modern theology is to vindicate
this vital doctrine, with its abstract notion of imputation,
and bold rejection of our partaking of the humanity of
Christ.

outward imputation of Christ's righteousness to
believers. According to Catholic theology, it is
the making us righteous by the regenerating
and sanctifying influence of the Spirit, which
Protestant theology has justly rejected. According to Oxford theology, or Puseyism (which
seeks to mediate between the Catholic and Protestant idea), justification is the making us
righteous by the communication of the divine
life of Christ, which, being divine and holy,
makes us righteous. According to Mercersburg
theology, the Protestant doctrine of imputation
is substantially correct, that we are accounted
righteous for the sake of the merits and righteousness of Christ (his active and passive obedience whilst on earth); but apprehends the doctrine more profoundly, by adding, that the
divine act of imputation in the case is condi-
tioned by our actual participation in these
merits, by virtue of our union with Christ. It
is not simply a declaratory, but a creative act
at the same time, which brings us into possession
of Christ's merits, which are imputed to us for

righteousness. The merits of Christ are therefore not, as modern theology would have it, simply set over to our account, but are made over to us in fact, in the mystical union of Christ and the believer. The merits of Christ are inseparable from his divine-human person or life, and go together in the simultaneous act of justification and regeneration, which do not follow each other in the order of time.*

§ 11.—REGENERATION.

Regeneration, according to modern theology, is, to use the most plausible form of expression, a change of heart, wrought by the operation of the Holy Spirit. To deny this is enough to cause men and women to raise up their hands in holy horror. According to Mercersburg theology, neither an outward reformation, nor an inward change of heart and mind, constitutes regeneration. These are but the *results* of regeneration,

---

* See notes 4 and 5.

not regeneration itself; the product simply of something that lies back of it, and deeper and profounder than all this. Regeneration, according to Mercersburg theology, is truly and really what the Saviour calls it, the new birth! This is a different idea altogether. It is not like changing a filthy garment into a clean one, which is the type of regeneration according to modern theology. There is, according to this view, much taken away from our old nature; but nothing new is added that was not at hand before the washing began. It is still our old nature—the old Adam—washed, and cleansed, and dressed up like a veritable-looking Christian, it is true; but he is, for all that, not a new creature. How different from all this is the prominent idea in the conception of a *New Birth*, or that of being made a new creature in Christ Jesus! What is implied in a natural birth? A life-communication; and the new birth is nothing short of this. It is, according to Mercersburg theology, the communication of Christ's life to believers, by the operation of the Holy Spirit.   Christ is to be formed within us, the hope of glory, and this life-communication is the beginning of the process; the end, our entire sanctification by the assimilating and transforming power of the life of Christ, which, by the operation of the Holy Spirit, becomes the life of our life, and more and more the life of our whole being, until our remaining corruption is finally and forever surmounted. The deepest ground of Christ's life, in the act of regeneration, enters into the deepest ground of our life, where they become one, the latter being raised up into the order and quality of the former; a parallel of which, to some extent, may be found in the grafted vine, which unites in one the life of the old vine and that of the new, whilst the life of the old vine is raised up into the nature and quality of the new.

------

§ 12.—THE NEW CREATION.

Regeneration is nothing more nor less than the new birth, and not itself, strictly speaking,

the new creation; but it has its ground in the
new creation. Man, at the head of the first
creation, with all its different orders of life, with
which he stood intimately and harmoniously
connected, stood in the same intimate and har-
monious relation with God, his creator, and the
paradise on earth with the paradise above. God
and man were united, heaven and earth were in
harmony. When man fell from this high estate,
he involved all nature in the ruin of his fall.
God and man were separated. Paradise was
lost, heaven and earth were parted. How can
this lost unity between God and man, between
the human and divine, the natural and the supernatural be again restored? Can what is
thus unhappily broken and separated be again
joined together, so as fully to answer its original
idea of unity? Modern theology says, *yes, certainly.* Mercersburg theology says, *no, never.*
Old things must pass away, and all things must
become new. A new creation is here wanted to
restore the *unbroken unity* which was lost. Any
thing short of this would be but the old crea-

tion patched up, a thing mended, but not made new, whether its joining together could be effected by screwing up and elevating the one part, or depressing the other, or by both. A thing once broken, however it may be joined together, can never be any thing more than an old mended thing. The divine nature lost in the fall of the race, cannot be restored, except by a new creation. It is only thus that God and man, heaven and earth, can again become united, and paradise restored on earth. The necessity of this, and the nature of this new creation, and its relation to the new birth, will become clearer to the mind by entering a little more into detail. Man, and with him all the lower kingdoms and orders of life in the first creation, fell from the life of God. The lowest order of life (if life it can be called*), is present in the mineral kingdom, which approximates to

---

* Dr. Hahneman's system of medicine rests on the theory, that there is in every particle of matter, a latent principle analogous to life, the manifestations of which are the effects it produces when brought into contact with organic life.

the vegetable kingdom, in which a higher order of life is manifestly present. This again approximates the animal kingdom, in which life and its manifestations are of a higher order still. This looks up and approximates a still higher order of life than itself, which is human life. All these different kingdoms and orders of life, stand intimately related to each other, and even flow into each other, so that it is difficult sometimes to draw the line of distinction; and yet each one, by the law of its nature, is limited to its own order of existence, and is not able to overleap its own boundary, and become something higher than itself. Here then we have these various kingdoms and orders of life: first the mineral, secondly the vegetable, then the animal, then the human. *Beyond* this, there is still a higher order of life, the divine life—but at what a distance beyond the human! Here is the open gap, caused by the fall. Originally this gap did not exist. Before the fall, man stood in as intimate relation to the divine life, as he stands to the orders of life beneath him.

But sin caused the separation. There is the breach. Man and this present world stand on one side, God and paradise on the other. Heaven and earth cannot be so moved as to bring them together. The case requires the actual creation of a new kingdom, and a new order of life to mediate between them. And what order of life is here wanted to fill up the chasm and re-unite them? Not a purely *human*, nor a purely *divine* order of life; for these are already at hand. The case requires a *divine-human* order of life, that will fit in, and fill up the gap. Such a divine-human life is provided for in the person and kingdom of our Lord Jesus Christ, the new creation, in which God and man, heaven and earth are again united. By the new birth we are born into this new kingdom, and become new creatures in Christ Jesus. By our natural birth we are born fallen and sinful beings, destitute of the life of God. The law of sin, which is the controlling law of this life, will never allow it to rise above itself. A mineral can never be cultivated into a vegetable, nor a vegetable into an animal, nor an animal trained into a human being, nor a sinner into a Christian. An ape may look very much like a human being, and be taught to play many human tricks, but he remains an ape for all that. And unless the sinner be born again, and become a new creature in Christ Jesus, he can never surmount the law of sin, which binds him to his fallen condition, *the life and order of mere nature.*

---

§ 13.—THE BODY OF CHRIST.

But the real difficulty in the way of modern theology is, after all, an old anthropological one, raised by ancient and revived by modern critics, which has brought into almost universal discredit the doctrine of our partaking of the humanity of Christ. These critics, both ancient and modern, have failed, however, to show, on truly scientific principles, that the doctrine of the Church, that believers partake of the body of Christ, is untenable; and it was entirely premature and fatal to all sound theological views, to drop this doctrine in our modern systems of theology. The objections of these false critics rest on the exploded assumption, that the human body is essentially and entirely *material*, and consequently governed by the laws of matter exclusively. We admit that the science of anthropology was not so far advanced at the time, that the ancient Church, or the Reformers in their day, were able to reply successfully to this objection;*and yet they held firmly to the doctrine thus assailed, because they found it contained in God's word and essential to the whole system of Christian doctrine. *Luther* endeavored to meet this objection, by taking the position, that, by virtue of the union of both natures in the person of Christ, his body, in a glorified state, could be present wherever his divinity was. However true this may be, when properly apprehended, it is neither correct nor satisfactory when predicated of the body of Christ as something in itself corporeal and exclusively material. *Calvin* felt this, and endeavored to solve the difficulty in another way.

According to his view, our faith elevates us above the limits and laws of space, and brings us thus into living union with his body, though he be in heaven and we on earth. However true this also is, when properly apprehended, it was equally unsatisfactory when predicated of things corporeal. It is true of things spiritual, but not of things material. But whether these different and well-meant attempts succeeded in satisfying the demands of reason or not, both Luther and Calvin and their respective followers, held firmly to the doctrine, that we partake of the body of Christ truly and really. Melancthon and the Heidelberg Catechism perhaps took the wisest course. They, too, taught the positive doctrine that we partake truly and really of the body of Christ as the teachings of God's word, which is higher than our poor, limited, and erring human reason; and left reason to get rid of the difficulty the best way it could, or to submit itself, as it is in duty bound, to the word of God. While thus both the Reformed and Lutheran Churches were united in holding to the doctrine in question, whilst they differed merely in their respective modes of explaining it, modern theology succumbed and gave up the contest, by giving up the doctrine itself. Instead of progressing and apprehending the doctrine more profoundly, theology retrograded and became itself rationalistic in order to square itself with such hyper-criticism. Mercersburg theology holds firmly to the doctrine of the Church, not only as sound and safe, but as essential to the maintenance of the whole system of Christian doctrine. It does so, not by ignoring the objections referred to, but by proving and exposing their fallacy. According to the anthropological conception, which underlies Mercersburg theology, the *accidental parts* of the human body, it is true, are material and subject to the laws of matter; but the *essential part* is spiritual, and not subject to these laws. We do not partake, for example, of the material substance of Adam's body, which has been mouldering in the grave for six thousand years;— and yet, notwithstanding this freely admitted fact, all his children, red, white and black, are bone of his bone and flesh of his flesh. More than this, we derive from him our whole nature, body, soul and spirit—but not, if you please, the bread and butter, the Indian corn and Irish potatoes, that enter at any time into the outward and material structure of the body. The *identity* of the body, its *true, essential and imperishable substance*, does not consist in any of these material accidents. The parallel being thus fully established, to which others could be added, there can be no really scientific objection raised against the doctrine, that believers partake of the body of Christ, the second Adam, who are bone of his bone and flesh of his flesh, by virtue of their new birth, as truly and really as they are of the first Adam, by their natural birth.

CHAPTER III.

§ 14.—THE SACRAMENTS.

SUFFICIENT has already been said, bearing on the sacramental question, and but little is required to be repeated here under its specific head. It is enough here to say, that according to Mercersburg theology, the Sacrament of Baptism is the divinely instituted means by which, ordinarily, the life-communication takes place, which, as already stated, is the beginning of that process, by which Christ is formed within us, the hope of glory; and that that life is especially fed and nourished by the Bread of life, communicated to us in the Sacrament of the body and blood of Christ. As modern theology has no conception of any such a life-communication at any time, and has given up the whole idea of our partaking of the body of Christ, under any form, it cannot admit that any thing of the kind takes place in the use of the sacraments. In being thus unsacramental, it is but consistent with its whole theory of Christianity and the Church.

---

§ 15.—THE ORGANIC LAW OF CHRISTIANITY.

The organic law of Christianity, as a higher order of life than any which is found in the sphere of mere nature, holds in its body, the Church, as primarily present, and proceeding from, the person of Christ. The Individualism of modern theology admits no such organic law in the case. The Church is, accordingly, in no real sense, an organic body; but a mere collection and organization of individual Christians, who adopt such Church polity as to them may seem to promote the general interests of Christianity under such form. But there is no binding force on the conscience of any one, to abide by the confederation thus formed. Each one is at liberty to break loose from it and join another, or start a new one, better suited to his fancy, without violating any principle except that, perhaps, of propriety and expediency. It is lawful, but may not be proper or expedient, is the extent of the restriction under which the radicalism, thus recognized as legitimate, is held; but as each individual is to be the judge of the expediency and propriety in his own case, the restriction amounts to nothing. Full license is thus given to the sect spirit, and is justified in the premises in breaking up the Church into as many fragments as it pleases. Hence, there is no Church authority that has a right to interfere in maintaining her integrity by restraining the conscience of men. No Church authority is recognized and respected except such as each individual chooses to invest the Church with; and when he takes that back, the Church has no longer jurisdiction over him. The idea of the Church is thus reduced to a perfect level with any other voluntary human organization. There is nothing in it that binds Christians together organically. The Christian life which each one

4

may be supposed to possess, he holds only in himself, and does not extend and reach over, organically, to the rest of the members of the same body.

According to Mercersburg theology, however, the very fact, that Christianity is a LIFE, and not a mere idea or doctrine, contradicts the whole theory of the Church, as here presented. The philosophy which underlies the proper idea of the Church, lays down as a universal proposition, *that all life is organic,* to which the Christian life can form no exception. This being true in the premises, it follows as equally true, that the Christian life is attained only by an organic process; and we have the idea of the Church as an Organism, starting in the person of Christ as its fountain, and developing itself as His mystical body, of which we are the members.

Of the correctness of the universal proposition referred to, any one can convince himself by a little reflection. Wherever there is life and its manifestation, there is an organism, in which it holds and is actually present in the world. This is true of every order of life, and in all the manifold forms in which its presence is known to exist. The life of the animalcule, though invisible to the naked eye, has its organism, as well as that of the monster beast of the field. The life of the most minutely small plants up to the giant oaks of the forest, have all their peculiar organisms.

Human life is organic, and the body is its organism. Destroy this body and its life must perish. Outside of its organism life can have no existence for the actual world around us.

Nor can life reproduce and multiply itself, except by an organic process. The farmer, in order to multiply his grain, must allow it to undergo an organic process of germination, of growth and development, until it has reproduced itself a hundred fold in the ripened corn in the ear.

All legitimate fruit is the result of an organic process. Apples and peaches are not made, but grow; not in the air, but on trees. Yankees know how to make wooden nutmegs, and the French understand how to make all sorts of artificial flowers and fruit, that look very pretty; but no one thinks of accepting them as genuine. The difference between the true and false is apparent—the one grows, the other is made. We have any number of such ready-made Christians in the world, whose Christianity is professedly not the result of any organic process.

The family is an organism, of which parents are the head and children the members. Children are not born outside and brought together into the family, but are born into this relation. All else are illegitimate and forfeit all claim to heirship. Bastard Christians are equally excluded from being heirs with the children of God.

The State is an organism, in which the life of the nation is embodied; and its laws, its institutions and citizenship, are the product of its organic life. Outside of this organic relation to the State, there can be no such thing as a citizen of the State. All others are aliens, whether in or outside of the State; and all who are not organically related to the Church are aliens to the commonwealth of Israel, the kingdom of Christ.

The Church is an organism, and embodies the highest and freest order of life. It is the body of Christ, and we are its members. By the process of organic development, the life of Christ has become the life of the Church, which is the bearer of His life, and the home of his presence in the world, to dispense life, and grace, and truth, to all who come unto Him. Outside of this organism there can be no Christians, no Christianity, because outside of it there is no Saviour, no life, no salvation for a lost and ruined world. All this is implied in the simple and undeniable fact, that Christianity is a life; for if it be a life at all, it is organic. The only escape from this is to deny that it is a life, and resolve it into mere idea or doctrine or precept, or any thing else; but this is falling helplessly into the arms of Rationalism and Infidelity.

§ 16.—THE CHURCH AS AN OBJECT OF FAITH.

The Church becomes accordingly an object of faith, inasmuch as it is a continuation of the mystery of the Incarnation, with which it stands connected as an article of faith in the Apostles' Creed. This continuation of the life of Christ in the Church, is as real as the life of the race is a continuation of the life of the first Adam; but like the mystery of the incarnation itself, it transcends all the laws of mere nature, and becomes an object of faith. According to modern theology, the Church is not an object of faith, and no mystery is connected with it. It has, accordingly, no sympathy with the Creed. The Church being but a voluntary association of Christians, outwardly brought together, without the binding tie of a common organic life, it becomes an object, not to be apprehended by faith, but by the baldest common sense.

---

§ 17.—THE CHURCH AND THE REFORMATION.

Mercersburg theology makes accordingly proper account of the ancient faith of the Church, as embodied in the Creed; as well as of the Church itself in all ages. Hence its invaluable productions in the department of Church history (vide Dr. Schaff's Church History). While it takes the position that Protestant theology is an advance over Catholic theology, it yet maintains that it is the reproduction of the latter under a deeper and profounder apprehension of its truths, and not the production of a new theology. So with the faith of the Church, and the Church itself. The Church of the Reformation, with its faith and doctrines, was not the product of any individual or number of individuals, who started fresh from the Bible in reconstructing the Church and its faith and doctrines. It was the result of the best life of the Catholic Church itself, which was tending and struggling toward this end for centuries, until it reached its culmination in the great Reformation.

Modern theology has no sense and appreciation for any such organic connection with the past history and life of the Church. Its study and labor in Church history is rather to find cause to be confirmed in its theory, the very opposite to this. The Reformation was, accordingly, not the result of a life-process, or historical development; but merely the work of individual men, who, finding the Church not to their idea, left it as the synagogue of Satan, and reconstructed a new one on what they considered to be the plain sense of the Bible, much in the same style in which this is attempted by modern sects. But this theory wrongs the Reformation in its most vital parts. It is virtually giving up the Reformation as a falling away; as the anti-Christian power that arrays itself against the mystery of the incarnation, of which the Church in all ages is its continuation in the world.

§ 18.—ROMANIZING TENDENCY.

According to modern theology, these teachings of Mercersburg would lead the Church back to Rome. But how, it has never been made to appear. Certainly not by the process of organic development, which never goes backward. Only individuals who are not comprehended in this organic process, go backward. The Church as an organism can never retrograde. All organic life is bound to go forward; and if Protestant Christianity is what Mercersburg theology contends for, it can never lead us back to Rome. The great danger lies precisely in the modern theory here brought to view. Earnest minds, who accept it as the true exposition of Protestantism, are inevitably carried over to Rome, to escape its logical consequences, that would ingulf them in the abyss of infidelity. The successful vindication of Protestantism depends, therefore, upon the successful refutation of this modern theory of the Church.

CHAPTER IV.

§ 19.—THE OFFICE OF THE MINISTRY.

THE office of the ministry, according to modern theology, is not invested with functions commensurate with the divine and supernatural facts and realities with which it has to deal, and in whose service it has been instituted. It has no power to bind the conscience of men in matters of faith and practice, being clothed with no binding power of any kind. However well a man may be accredited as a minister of Jesus Christ, he is, in no real sense, the organ through which Christ speaks, whose words and official acts are to be accepted in good faith, as being in accordance with his instructions. Instead of such faith in his favor, or rather in favor of the truth he répresents, in the premises, he must allow those to whom he is accredited, the advantage of entertaining a doubt in what he says, until he convinces them by documentary or other evidences, that he is not misrepresenting the truth, of which they themselves are to be the judges. He has, accordingly, no right to expect, for instance, that even the children of the Church should believe the Creed, until he has convinced their understanding, that its contents agree with the teaching of the Bible; and not even to believe in the Bible itself, until he has proved to them that it is the word of God; and that God's Word is something which they must accept by faith unconditionally, without asking any farther troublesome questions. But as he is not allowed to make any such demand in the premises, he will have some considerable difficulty to find the point where the unconditional faith comes in spontaneously, from which he can proceed to build them up in the faith and knowledge of the truth.

This whole view of the office of the ministry

is humiliating and degrading, both to Christ and his ministers. The common courtesies of life are denied to a minister the moment he speaks and acts in his official capacity. Nothing that he says or does as an accredited minister of Christ, is to be received in good faith. There is nothing in the dignity and character of his office, or in his relation to the Church and to Christ, or in the nature and substance of the message he is commissioned to deliver, that should demand such faith in the premises. He has literally nothing to fall back upon, to inspire faith in them that hear him. He must be ready to prove every word and act of his, before it is accepted as being true. No premises are admitted, from which he may choose to start, and he is brought to a dead lock at once. He must cease proclaiming the gospel, and enter the domain of philosophical speculation as a last resort, to find, if possible, an admitted premise, which involves the whole system of truth which he is commissioned to preach. Christ is not himself the truth, and the truth is not to be found in Him, nor in His Word, nor in His Church; but somewhere in the interminable depth of philosophical speculations, where it has been sought in vain for four thousand years, until it appeared in the flesh in the person of Christ, who commissioned His ministers to preach it—not to prove it; to proclaim it—not to demonstrate it.

According to Mercersburg theology, the Church embodies a continuation of the life of Christ on earth, and the office of the ministry is a continuation of His prophetic, His priestly and kingly office. If Christ be present in the Church, as His mystical body, He is not only present in His divine and human nature, but also in His threefold office, with their divine and supernatural functions. That office, with its functions, is reproduced in the office of the ministry, which He Himself instituted and solemnly invested, with the promise to be identified with it to the end of time. The office of the ministry thus stands in living, organic, and immediate relation to Christ, as prophet, priest, and king. The prophetic, priestly, and kingly office, as foreshadowed in the old dispensation, and fully realized in the person of Christ, is thus carried forward and perpetuated in the Christian Church. The Church, thus invested with the prophetic office, becomes, through her ministry, the teacher of mankind, and all men are bound to accept by faith, the words of eternal life, which it is commissioned to proclaim.

When the apostles preached the gospel, men were expected to receive it by faith, not blindly, by any means, but just as little on the ground of any extrinsic evidence lying beyond itself, but was backed by the demonstration of the divine and supernatural presence, by which their teachings were inspired. The divine and supernatural, which thus formed the basis on which their teachings were accepted by faith, continues present in the Church for all time to come, as the ever-abiding and immovable basis on which men now, and in all past and future ages, accept, by faith, the teachings of the gospel—the Bible, as being the word of God, included. The Church is thus, what the Bible affirms it to be, the pillar and ground of the truth.

---

§ 20.—OBJECTIVE FAITH.—THE CREED.

With these premises in her favor, the Church has a right to give formal expression to her faith, and to challenge its acceptance unconditionally. The Bible itself is an object of faith, and its contents can only be properly understood in the light of that faith which we receive from the Church. In the light of that faith, which we bring to it, do the internal evidences of the sacred Scriptures carry with them their full and legitimate force in confirming and establishing what has thus been apprehended by faith. Without such faith in the premises, the internal evidences of the Bible would fail to establish its own authenticity and inspiration, and no ground could be gained for faith to rest upon. We receive our faith from the Church, as expressed, for instance, in the Apostles' Creed, and must bring that faith with us, and in the light of it, read the Bible, in order to understand its contents—*the contents of our faith, as well as the Bible*, which is, to us Protestants, the only infallible norm of that faith, as the God-given safeguard against the possible aberration from the truth.

Modern theology makes no account of the Creed. It has no power to appreciate its intrinsic worth, or its catholicity and historical value. It is, in fact, of no manner of value in a system of theology, *that starts without faith in any thing!* It does not need the universal faith of the Church as a starting-point. Its own private judgment can get along well enough without it. It gets its faith fresh from the Bible, which is superior to any old and musty creeds of the Church, which only hamper the free exercise of a more enlightened judgment. But we have already seen the dead lock, to which even a little child can bring it, when forced to make good its flippant and silly pretensions.

Mercersburg theology does not hesitate to acknowledge that it stands in full sympathy with the universal faith of the Church, as expressed in the Creed. It is of infinite importance to find such universally admitted premises, from which we can proceed in building up the Church in the faith and knowledge of the truth. Here is something to start upon; something that challenges our acceptance, on the ground that it has been admitted by the universal Church in all ages. What an advantage this in the catechisation and instruction of children in a communion where proper account is made of the Creed! It is, besides, a bond of union, that still binds all Christians together in the unity of a common faith, which all their dire conflicts and divisions could not destroy. This is itself a stupendous fact, challenging implicit faith, that what has under such circumstances been universally and in all ages held as true, must be true indeed. It is only equalled by the same unanimity with which the Bible has been accepted as the word of God, which is the normative rule of faith, as expressed in the Creed. And, as such, they

5

cannot be separated. They stand or fall together. As long as the Creed is accepted as an expression of our undoubted Christian faith, the Bible will be accepted as the undoubted word of God, and as long as the Bible is revered as the undoubted word of God, will the Creed be revered as our undoubted Christian faith.

There is a necessary and inseparable relation between Creed and Bible, without an implied co-ordination. The Creed is the expression of our undoubted Christian faith, the Bible the undoubted and infallible norm of its contents. Separate them, and you destroy the unity of faith on the one hand, and reject the Bible as its infallible rule on the other. If we set aside the Creed, we give up our common faith; and if we go to gather our faith fresh from the Bible, we shall have as many different kinds of faith as there are different apprehensions of its contents. The Bible is no longer the infallible rule of an undoubted and universally accepted faith, but is made the rule for any number of conflicting kinds of faith (falsely so called), which is but a mockery of both faith and the word of God. Both suffer alike, and the inevitable result of such a separation, would be the rejection of both.

Modern theology is unwittingly paving the way for just such a sad result; and the miserable sect-system which it encourages, is hatching out a brood of skeptics and infidels, who will learn to despise the authority of the Bible with as much zeal as they are now taught to despise the authority of the Church.

But the Creed should be cherished for still another reason. It is not only important as reaching back through all past ages of the Church, but is looking forward in the future-Being the bond that still holds Christians to. gether in the unity of their common faith, it only requires to make proper account of this fact, to find that the Creed is the basis and starting-point for the future unity of the Church, which we all so ardently desire.

CHAPTER V.

§ 21.—RULE OF FAITH.

MERCERSBURG theology accepts, without reservation, the old Protestant doctrine, that the Bible is the only infallible rule of faith; but rejects the modern perversion of this doctrine, that it is the only source of faith. According to modern theology, we derive our faith directly from the Bible, and the rule of our faith, to be derived from it, is every man's private judgment. *That,* and not the *Bible,* is the only infallible rule of faith, according to modern theology. It reverses the order of faith and knowledge. Our faith is made to rest on what we know or understand to be the teachings of the Bible, according to which there are as many different kinds of faith as there are different apprehensions of the teachings of the Bible.

According to Mercersburg theology, we must believe in order to understand. Whatever effect knowledge may have to confirm and strengthen our faith, faith embraces always, from first to last, something more and deeper, than our knowledge of its contents. We may have faith, but may not have the knowledge of all it includes, and all that it excludes. The rule of faith determines this, as far as its contents can be known. We derive our faith from the Church—from the rule of faith our knowledge of its contents. We bring that faith with us, when we go to the Bible as the rule of faith, and in the light of both we learn to understand more and more their sense and meaning.

But let it be remembered, that the Bible is given to the Church as the rule of faith, and that she has brought her faith to it and studied it for centuries. The accumulated knowledge or apprehension of its truth, thus reached, has, from time to time, been reduced into regular order and system, which constitutes the theology of the Church. We thus not only receive our faith from the Church, but the most of what we really know and understand of the teachings of the Bible. For an individual to sit in judgment over the faith and doctrines of the Church, with nothing but an open Bible before him, *with no previous faith* in his heart, and nothing but his *private judgment* in his noddle, is simply an arrogant presumption, which exalts individual conceit above the faith, the wisdom and intelligence of the whole Church, past and present.

The progressive development of theological science, or a clearer and profounder apprehension of the doctrines of Christianity, is an important part of the organic development of the life of the Church, and is not the product, in any way, of independent individualism, which has never contributed any thing positive in settling a single point in theological science; but is capable only of reproducing old errors under new forms, whose fallacies have been exposed time and again.

§ 22.—THE SACRED SCRIPTURES.

Mercersburg theology is also free to admit, that the Bible carries within itself the evidence of being the word of God. But to what does it authenticate itself as the word of God? Is it to faith, or to the understanding? We know by faith, that the Bible is the word and truth of God, and not otherwise. It is as much an object of faith as any thing else that is divine and supernatural. That the Bible is God's word and truth is self-evident to faith, and to faith alone. There is that in it, which fully harmonizes and meets the wants of our spiritual nature, which accepts it as truth on its bare presentation. It does not argue and reason on the subject. It does not require any proof, as little as any other self-evident truth does. The Bible is to faith the word of God, independent, in fact, of all internal and external proof. It is accepted as we accept any other self-evident truth or universal proposition.

If the position of modern theology, however, be taken, that the Bible must first authenticate itself to the understanding, before we can accept it and believe in it as the word of God, then it is reduced to the nature of a minor proposition, that requires to be established by proof. Whether the proof may be found inside or outside of its pages, is all the same—it has to be produced, and be satisfactory to the understanding. The proof, of course, must be such as can be comprehended by the understanding, which thus sits in judgment in the case. The *deeper, inner, spiritual sense* which runs through the Bible from beginning to end, cannot be brought in as evidence in the case, because it is beyond the grasp of the bare understanding. The very evidence on which its authentication depends, is thus ruled out in deciding the question for faith, whether the Bible be the word of God.

Strange that any professed Christian should be willing to let the trial go on before such an incompetent tribunal, and accept the results as the ground of his faith in the Bible! And yet this is precisely what modern theology and what undisguised Rationalism are doing. We will say nothing in regard to which is the more consistent in its conclusions. It is enough to know, that they arrive at very different results, which involves the question in sufficient doubt and uncertainty to justify us in rejecting their premises. But no such different and opposite conclusions are arrived at **by** those who apprehend the Bible by *faith*. No one who has ever apprehended the deeper, inner, spiritual sense of the Bible, has come to any other conclusion, than that it is the word and truth of God; and no one has ever thrown a shadow of doubt on this point. They may differ in comprehending its contents in detail, or in all its heights and depths, according to the measure of faith given unto them; but as to its divine origin and truth, they are a cloud of witnesses that proclaim it with one universal accord.

§ 23.—SUBJECTIVE FAITH.

It is a comfort to know, that men's faith is often better than their theology; so that while we are bound to reject their views and theories on faith, we can afford to admit, that they may not be destitute of faith itself. It is what Mercersburg theology contends for, that our understanding of spiritual things is not their measure and criterion. But to entertain and cherish views of spiritual things contrary to their nature, is, to say the least of it, extremely dangerous; especially to those who *do* make their understanding of spiritual things the rule and measure of their contents. This holds true in reference to all matters of faith, but especially in reference to *faith itself*, which is an object of *self-apprehension;* that is, faith must apprehend itself, and reveal its nature to the understanding, in order to have any rational conception of it. Where there is no such self-apprehension of faith, the understanding can have no conception of its nature, and its views on the subject are mere conjectures and speculations, which satisfy neither the heart nor the understanding, because they are destitute of that certitude which we have a right to expect in a proposition on so important a subject.

In reversing the order of faith and knowledge, as is done by modern theology, *faith itself is made to be something very different from what it is in reality.* The question of order here involves two radically different views of faith itself, so widely different. indeed, that they are virtually made to exclude each other.

According to Mercersburg theology, there is in the constitution of man's higher and spiritual nature, an innate power of apprehending spiritual and divine things, which, when excited into exercise by the lively preaching of the gospel, or by being brought into immediate and proper relation to divine and spiritual realities, constitutes *Faith.* By the exercise of this power "he enters into communion with the invisible and spiritual world; into the heart and mind of God himself, and draws from thence new spiritual

life for his own being."* However deeply
fallen and depraved, our higher nature is still
conscious of its divine origin, and longs for re-
union and re-communion with God, and the
spiritual world from which it sprung. Like the
prodigal son, the type of the Gentile world, that
lives without God, it cannot be totally lost to
the consciousness that God is its father and a
lost paradise its proper home, for which it longs
and sighs, in the midst of the beggarly elements
of this present world.

Modern theology, on the contrary, proceeds
on the assumption, that there is no such inherent
power in man. Whether it assumes the infidel
position, that he never had a spiritual nature,
grounded in the constitution of his being, or the
position, that it was entirely lost by the fall, it
amounts to the same thing. He has not that
nature now, and no such power is inherent in
him by which he can apprehend spiritual things.
He must accordingly apprehend them, if at all,

---

* Dr. Nevin.

not by any spiritual, but by the intellectual powers of his being, and thus know, before he can believe. He must be taught to know that there is a God, on evidences that convince his understanding, before he can believe there is a God, and so on to the end of the chapter. But such *belief* in God, is something very different from *faith* in God. The truth of God is not revealed to faith, but to the understanding; and the intellectual assent of the mind to the truth thus presented and apprehended, constitutes faith. But, contingent on mere evidence, it must ever be a very uncertain and doubtful faith, liable to be driven about by every wind of doctrine, because it lacks that certitude which true faith implies, and which no amount of mere proof, nor evidence, nor logical reasoning can ever produce. It is not itself the evidence or authentication of things not seen, but rests on evidences lying wholly beyond itself and aside of the object on which it is exercised. We shall reserve our concluding remarks on this point, and embody them in a separate section on the

NATURE OF EVIDENCES, in which we shall give, with the indulgence of the reader, a few simple and familiar illustrations of a subject involving perhaps the most important points of difference between the two systems under consideration; and, at the same time, by implication, the radical difference between Mercersburg and Rome.

CHAPTER VI.

§ 24.—ON THE NATURE OF EVIDENCES.

ACCORDING to modern theology, faith is the assent of the mind to the truth, on the conviction produced by the force or authority of evidences. There is, substantially, no difference between this position and that of Rome. The premises are the same, and they differ only with respect to the kind of evidence or authority, which is accepted as credible and satisfactory. In both cases faith is assent to an established truth, established by recognized authority. According to Mercersburg theology, faith is the apprehension of a *self-evident* truth, that requires no proof or authority beyond itself. The result on the heart and mind is not the same. In the one case a *moral* certainty is established;

in the other an *absolute* certainty. This important difference lies, primarily, in the *nature of things* and *our relation to them.*

Facts that surround us, and with which we have to deal, are of two kinds,—*transient* and *continuous.* The truth of the former is far more difficult to reach than that of the latter. Existing but for a time, and often but momentarily, transient facts are evident to but few, who can bear testimony in reference to them; while continuous facts are permanently evident to all who take the trouble to examine them. Hence the truth of the former has to be established by evidence, while the latter do not require this, being self-evident. We shall give an example of both, and then see how they apply to the greatest of all facts—Christianity.

"*John struck Peter.*" This declaration assumes one of those transient facts, which require to be established by proof or evidence, before its truth can be assented to by the mind. As a mere proposition or assertion, we can neither believe it nor reject it. It may be or may not be true, that John did so bad a thing as to strike Peter. Who knows? James and Isaac know, who saw it; and they testify to its truth. As they are credible witnesses, we accept their testimony as evidence, and on the strength or authority of it, believe that John did commit the assault on Peter. There is a reasonable and moral certainty established that such is the fact, and the criminal law adjudges him guilty, and the moral law approves the finding.

But we, who hear and believe this testimony, and join in the verdict, have not that certitude of the fact, which would enable us to venture our salvation on its truth, by taking an oath that John did strike Peter. There is no reasonable doubt that he did. We are morally certain of it, on the authority of unquestionable testimony; but there is no *absolute* certainty established; and no amount of evidence can do this. *It is not in the nature of proof or evidence to do it.* The moral or reasonable certainty reached by such a process, can never, of itself, or by any amount of additional proof, rise to absolute certainty. When you come to define it, it is, and never can be any thing more than, *belief*. Only those who *know* that John struck Peter (the witnesses in the case), have an absolute certainty of the fact; and they did not get their knowledge of the fact by any such a process.

Hence it is that human judgment and courts of justice are liable to err, even when declarations are established beyond all reasonable doubt. They *know* nothing of the facts themselves, but judge according to the evidence in the case. But all things are known to God, and, therefore, there can be no error in His judgment. He stands so immediately related to all things by His omnipresence, that He Himself is witness to them, even the secret thoughts and intentions of the heart.

We know nothing but what is, or can be made self-evident to us, and only those, to whom the truth is thus known in any case, are competent to bear testimony to the truth. A man who would present himself as a witness, that John struck Peter, because he heard others say so, or swear to it, would be laughed at and sent about his business.

This is but a simple case, but it illustrates an important principle. *It shows us the nature of evidences,* and what they can and what they cannot establish;—that by their means we can come to a belief, *but not to a knowledge of the truth;* and that, unless we possess this knowledge by reaching it in some other way, we are not qualified to bear witness to the truth. But let us consider the next case.

"The sun shines." This is not a transient, but a continuous fact. The sun shone in the days of the Apostles, and it shines in our days. If needs be, the truth of this can be established by evidence; because there are credible witnesses who can testify to the fact. As clear a case can be made out in this way as the one we have just considered, to say the least of it. But it needs no proof. It is not on trial before a court and jury; and if it be, we do not wait to hear their verdict, whether it shines or not. We know it,

and in advance of all such proceedings, and all arguments and reasoning on the subject. We know it, because it is self-evident to all who will open their eyes and look at it. A man who has no eyes, or who has them, but cannot see, must, of course, accept it on the testimony or authority of others. On the strength of that, he may believe, but does not know that the sun shines. Such mere evidence, or mere authority and belief, does not give eyes to the blind. It does the poor man no good. It does not open his eyes, and enable him to see the sun; which is the necessary condition on which the sun can be of any benefit to him.

Here, then, we have the two cases before us. The first is a case, the truth of which is accepted on the simple authority of those, who are admitted to know the facts; or by submitting the case to a regular process of examination into the evidences, on which its truth can be established;— but all of which leads nobody to a *knowledge* of the truth. The other is a case, in which every body who will, can come to a knowledge of the truth, in advance and independent of such a process. Both cases are equally clear, and a bare presentation of them is sufficient to make them self-evident to the mind.

But how do these two cases apply to the greatest of all facts, Christianity?

To those who are for ever in search of the truth by the process indicated in the first case, the words, in a modified but true sense apply: "Ever learning, and never able to come to a knowledge of the truth." 2 Tim. iii. 7. And the words: "If any man think that he knoweth any thing (by that process), he knoweth nothing yet as he ought to know." 1 Cor. viii. 2.

To those who come to a knowledge of the truth on the principle indicated in the second case, the words of the Samaritans, addressed to a witness of Jesus, apply: "Now we believe, not because of thy saying: for we have heard him ourselves, and know that he is indeed the Christ, the Saviour of the world." John iv. 42.

Christianity is not a transient fact, like the case of John and Peter; but a continuous and

permanent fact, like that of the sun, or the everlasting hills. As such its truth can be established on the authority of the most unquestionable evidences; but its truth does not rest and
depend on any kind or any amount of mere evidences; but is open to the immediate apprehension of all who come to stand in immediate relation to it, and bring with them the power of apprehending it—faith—to which it is self-evident
on its bare presentation.

We have already admitted that a clear case
can be established, that the sun shone in the
days of the Apostles, and that it shines to this
day, by any amount of credible testimony. So
has the truth of Christianity been proved a thousand times beyond all reasonable doubt, as much
so as any other truth has ever been established
by evidence. And in the absence of any evidence to the contrary, the man, who pretends to
deny it, is either a fool or a knave. He cannot,
as a sane and an honest man, even deny the truth
that John struck Peter, after hearing the testimony in the case. He is compelled to believe it.

But this is not exactly what is wanted, and not the kind of faith which Christianity demands and calls for, and which the preaching of the gospel (the bare presentation or proclamation of its truth) is intended to produce. A man wants to know for himself, that the sun shines, without which the sun can be of no benefit to him. All the authority, and testimony and argument in the world do not give him that knowledge of the fact, which a single glance at the sun would afford. The knowledge of the truth for which the soul longs and desires, is not obtained by any such a process of heaping evidence upon evidence from reason, from Scripture, from history, or from any where else. It is only obtained by being brought into immediate relation to the truth itself. The faith which apprehends Christianity as absolutely true, is not the cold intellectual assent of the mind, which is given in the case of John and Peter; but the exercise of a perceptive power, to which that truth becomes self-evident; and by which we know even more certainly that it is the truth, than James and

Isaac know that John struck Peter, or than any one of us knows, that the sun shines, from the evidences of our senses.

Mere belief, such as we have seen to result from evidence of proof in the case of John and Peter, or in the case of the blind man, who believes that the sun shines on the authority and testimony of others,—*is not faith,* that mysterious power in man, which apprehends the spiritual and invisible, and which gives us a greater certitude even than the evidences of our senses. We know that the sun shines, which is *external* and *visible* to the eye; but we know still more certainly, that we possess an *internal* and *invisible* power, which enables us to see the sun, and to discern it, and to know, that what is thus taken in by the senses, is not a delusion, a vision and a dream. By means of the eye, as the organ of the power of vision, we *see* the sun shine. By means of something lying back of that power, we *know* that it shines. That power we call *faith* (or if you prefer the term, our *higher reason*), the ultimate ground to which *all* our knowledge must be referred. Even the second-hand or indirect knowledge gained in the case of John and Peter, and the whole process of reasoning required to reach it, rest *ultimately* on faith; existing both in the *witnesses*, who testify on oath, and in the *judges* in the case, who have faith in the validity of that oath. Without faith in the credibility of witnesses, or *faith in the premises*, nothing can be proved, nothing established even to a reasonable certainty. All would be doubt and confusion. Reason itself would be dethroned. Courts of justice and equity would cease to exist, and the whole social fabric would fall to pieces, for the want of that binding force which holds it together, that mysterious power, *faith*, the foundation of reason itself, the ground and life-spring of all its powers and activities.

Christianity is an object of faith in the sense here presented. Its glorious truth can only be known and be of any real benefit to man, when apprehended as self-evident to faith; as in the case of the sun, which can be of benefit only to

those who see it. Without the absolute certainty
of its truth, which faith in it implies, its light
would not be a guide to our feet.   We would be,
spiritually, in the condition of the blind man,
and could not, from our knowledge of its truth,
bear witness and proclaim, that Christianity is
the true religion; that Christ is the Saviour of
the world; that he is the Son of God.   Our conviction, derived from mere testimony, would not
enable us to do this.   James and Isaac, on the
contrary, do not hesitate to declare, that John
struck Peter, and do not hesitate for a moment
to venture their salvation on its truth, by taking
a solemn oath to that effect—and why?   Because they know it to be the truth.   But the
mere lawyer, the judge and the jury, cannot do
this.   They cannot thus venture their salvation
on the conviction and knowledge of the truth
from evidence alone, however strong and unquestionable the authority may be, on which the evidences rest.   And how could a Christian minister and a Christian people venture their salvation on the truth of Christianity, if they did not

know more about it, than such mere evidences afford? Christianity itself demands of us, to venture our salvation upon it, by accepting it as our only hope in life and death. But such a demand would neither be just nor reasonable, if the absolute certainty of its truth and reliability could not be gained: as little as it would be just and reasonable to allow a man to take a solemn oath, that John struck Peter, who was not, from his own personal knowledge, absolutely certain that such was the fact. The ground of our hope, upon which we can venture our salvation, must be susceptible of becoming absolutely certain and reliable. Those who venture into the eternal world without this certitude, go into it blind, and will remain ingulfed in darkness for evermore. Their belief, which did them no good in this life, will do them no good in the world to come. It failed to lead them to a knowledge of the truth here; it will fail to do so hereafter.

All who can bear testimony to the truth, that the sun shines, are living witnesses, at the same time, that all who will exercise their power of

vision, can know it for themselves. The witnesses of Jesus, in all ages, have testified to the
same thing in reference to our holy Christianity.
The writings of the Apostles are full of it; the
martyrs for the truth have joyfully sealed it
with their blood; the dying saints have triumph-
antly confessed it; every true minister of the
gospel is a witness to its truth; and all true believers join with one accord in the confession of
the Samaritans: "Now we believe, not because
of thy saying; for we have heard him ourselves,
and know that this is indeed the Christ, the
Saviour of the world."

Christianity is a fact; not a transient, but a
continuous fact. As such, it is self-evident, not
to every body, but to those who apprehend it by
faith. We do not, therefore, claim for Christianity any thing that is not included in the
premises, when we say, that it is an object of
faith. We make the same claim in favor of all
other continuous facts. Faith in Christianity,
while it does emphatically differ from mere
natural *belief*, does not, in itself, differ from

natural faith. Psychologically considered, faith is of the same nature, whether its object is the natural or the supernatural. By mere belief, we know literally nothing (as we ought to know). What little we do know (in the proper sense of the word), we know by faith, because it is apprehended as self-evident by faith, whether it comprehends a natural or a supernatural truth, both of which have their ultimate ground in God. We have no right to refuse our assent to, much less reject *any thing*, whether natural or supernatural, human or divine, because, forsooth, we cannot arrive at an absolute certainty of its truth by the mere process and evidence of reason. Whether the truth of any thing is susceptible of becoming absolutely certain to us, depends upon whether it is susceptible of becoming self-evident. We have accordingly no right in the premises to reject the claim in favor of any fact which professes to be thus susceptible, and thus prejudge it in advance. In order to determine whether its claims are according to truth, we must test those claims. We must accordingly allow Christianity to make what claims it pleases, and try it on the merits of those claims. It claims to be an object of faith; an object that is susceptible to become self-evident, and its truth and reliability to become absolutely certain. To test this claim fairly, we are bound in all honesty and sincerity to place ourselves into such immediate relation to it, by which it may, if true, become thus self-evident to faith. Millions upon millions have done this in godly sincerity and child-like simplicity, and all, with one accord, testify to its truth; while those who reject Christianity *have never done this.* Hence it is, that the truth of God is revealed to child-like faith, and not to the pride of human reason. If anybody wants to know to what straits infidels have been driven as their last resort, by the force of that higher reason which Christianity inspires and has wielded against their infidelity, it is enough to say, that they now reject the truth of Christianity for the same reason, that they reject the truth of every thing besides.

They professedly *believe nothing*, and consequently acknowledge that they *know nothing*. But how they happen to know even this, is as great a mystery as any thing they intend to deny; for the hardest passage of Scripture for an infidel to admit to be true, is that of their strongest antagonist, who says, in speaking of such pretenders to wisdom: "*Professing themselves to be wise, they became fools.*" And now, since infidels virtually admit this, it is time that infidelity and its trade be abandoned. Both have expended themselves.

CHAPTER VII.

---

§ 25.—THE PULPIT—PREACHING.

ACCORDING to modern theology, as seen all along, every thing has to be proved in order to produce what is mistaken for faith, *belief*. The preacher is accordingly in the position of the lawyer, whose business it is to state his case to the judgment of his audience, to furnish his evidences and argue the case, in order to produce conviction in the minds of those who hear him. This being the great end and object of the Pulpit, he is educated and prepared mainly with a view of becoming an able minister in the sense here presented. He is considered the ablest minister accordingly, who can compress the greatest intellectual treat into his sermon bearing on the truth of his proposition, which he strives to prove and establish, by all the evidences, the arguments and eloquence of an intellect of the first capacity—no matter whether a single word be addressed to faith and the heart, or not; for it is not with the heart, but with the intellect that men believe unto righteousness, according to the theory of religion on which such preaching and its theology are based. Our higher spiritual nature is entirely ignored, and no attempt is made to present the gospel to *its* apprehension.

According to Mercersburg theology, the true idea of preaching the gospel is, to proclaim it, not to prove it; to let it speak for itself, not to defend it; to teach and explain it, not to declaim about it—in a word, to present it as self-evident to faith, to our higher spiritual nature, not to reduce it to the apprehension of the bare understanding. The *first* great business of the preacher is to open the eyes of the blind—those spiritual eyes blinded by sin—by applying the gospel to *them*, until man wakes up to his proper

7

self-consciousness, which implies a consciousness of his higher spiritual nature: the God-consciousness within him: the consciousness of sin and guilt; the consciousness of the need of redemption; the sense of justice, of holiness; the longing and desires of the heart for re-union and re-communion with God and the Paradise which is not found in the beggarly elements of this present world;—in other words, to lay open to him the higher law of his own nature, that speaks to him of his divine origin, of a God of justice, of righteousness, of a judgment to come, of the need of reconciliation, of pardon, of redemption, of longings for re-union with God and a world of future happiness;—and then, in the *second* place, reveal to this higher nature— these opened spiritual eyes—the God in Christ, the story of the fall, the story of redemption, and the Paradise regained and re-established in the kingdom of Christ;—and show how fully the revelations and provisions of the gospel explain and meet all the wants, the desires and longings of that better, higher nature. The gospel, thus

applied and presented immediately to our spiritual nature, becomes self-evident to it, and is apprehended by faith, which gives us an absolute
certainty of its truth, which no amount of evidence and argument addressed to the understanding or logical reason, can ever produce.

§ 26.—THE ALTAR.—WORSHIP.

To awaken man to his proper self-consciousness, it is not enough to *preach;* but it is
necessary also to *pray*, that God's Spirit may
aid in the work; for without Him we can do
nothing. . Hence, according to Mercersburg
theology, the Altar, as well as the Pulpit, finds
its appropriate place and significance in the
house of God. In coming to hear the word
preached, man must be made to feel that he is
coming to the house of God, which is the house
of prayer; and the more deeply he is impressed with this feeling, and the more solemnly
the worship of God is conducted, and confession
of sin and the Christian faith is made and de-

voutly responded to, the more deeply will he be
affected by an invisible presence, that thus aids
in awakening in him the slumbering consciousness of his own spiritual nature, by which he
becomes better prepared to hear and receive
the gospel addressed to him from the Pulpit.
What is true here in reference to him who is yet
out of Christ, is equally true of the Christian,
who is to be built up in the faith and knowledge
of the truth, by the same divinely appointed
means.

Modern theology, ignoring man's higher spiritual nature, is but consistent with itself, when
it ignores the Altar and its solemn services, and
puts it entirely out of the house of God! What
public worship there is, is done in the pulpit and
the end gallery by a choir of undevout young
people, who sing undevotional hymns to undevotional tunes; and the prayer in the pulpit
partakes of the undevotional smartness and in-
tellectualism, which characterize the whole service, preaching and all. The singing, the pray-
ing, the preaching, and the hearing are all by

the understanding and for the understanding—
not by the spirit and heart, and for them. Even
the central idea of worship, the holy sacrament
of the body and blood of Christ, is reduced to
the same common level of the mere understanding. There is nothing in the whole service, from
beginning to end, for immediate faith to lay hold
upon. Every thing is calculated to produce *belief*, or something less valuable than that; but
nothing is calculated to produce *faith*.

§ 27.—THE KEYS.—DISCIPLINE.

According to Mercersburg Theology, the
ministry combines not only the prophetic and
priestly, but also the kingly office of Christ, to
which the keys of the kingdom of heaven are
given for substantially the same purpose for
which its prophetic and priestly functions are
intended; namely, to bring men to a proper
sense or consciousness of their relation to God,
and divine and spiritual things. By virtue of

this office, the minister of Christ is clothed to speak and act with divine authority in rebuking sin and comforting believers. When exercised, as it ever should be, in the same spirit of an assured faith in which the prophetic and priestly functions are to be exercised and addressed, and applied to the same higher nature in man, it has an additional powerful effect to aid in awakening it to proper consciousness. How reviving and strengthening to the penitent's trembling faith, and comforting to the troubled spirit are, for instance, the solemnly uttered words of comfort and assurance coming from the lips of a minister of Christ, who speaks with conscious authority in the name of God. The Gospel of our salvation, thus applied to man's spiritual nature, by the proper exercise of the prophetic, priestly and kingly functions of the ministry, will prove "a power of God unto salvation to all them that believe, to the Jew first and also to the Greek."

Modern theology has explained away all divine and immediate force in this function of the ministry, as well as in that of the others. Its exercise carries with it no immediate force to the conciousness of man. Its cold comfort addressed to the understanding and intelligence, does not reach and comfort the troubled spirit and heal the broken heart. Its intellectual comfort is nothing but untempered mortar, and the penitent and mourning soul leaves the house of God with no assurance of faith and no solid comfort, to seek it elsewhere the best way it can, or remain without it.

§ 28.—CONFIRMATION.

According to Mercersburg theology, the rite of confirmation, or laying on of hands, is one of those ministerial acts, which is divinely intended to confirm and strengthen the faith of the believer. In baptism we are brought into covenant and gracious relation to God, and after the consciousness of this relation is properly developed by the hearing of the word (catechisation), it is confirmed and ratified by the laying on of hands, as the completion of the rite of baptism, as initiatory to full communion with the Church, and preparatory to admission to the Lord's table, all of which have the great object in view of awakening and strengthening a full assurance of faith or conscious union and communion with God in Christ Jesus.

Modern theology is here again consistent with itself, when it rejects the rite of confirmation as useless. It adds nothing to strengthen *mere belief*. If faith is nothing more than an intellectual assent of the mind, then of course the laying on of hands has nothing to do in producing or confirming it. But the same is equally true with regard to baptism and the Lord's supper. They do not and are not intended to produce or confirm *belief*, and might just as well be rejected as the Altar and the laying on of hands, for aught effect they have in convicting the *mere understanding*. To appreciate the sense and meaning of Confirmation, it must be viewed in the light of *faith*, as must every thing else connected with the Gospel.

According to modern theology and its practical application, the reception or recognition of a person in full communion and membership with the Christian Church, is not to be performed and signalized by any solemn ministerial act, as carrying with it any spiritual force and meaning to the faith and consciousness of the person admitted. He is simply acknowledged as a full member of the Church on confession of his belief, so that it may be *understood* by all whom it may concern, that he is entitled to all the rights and privileges of full membership. Here, again, all is simply for the understanding, and nothing for faith. His admission into the Church, has not brought him into a nearer or more conscious relation to Christ and the kingdom of God, than he had been in before. He has simply "joined the Church," as he would any other purely human association, and when he becomes tired of it, will "leave the Church" with as little conscious loss as he had of any conscious gain in "joining" it.

§ 29.—THE WITNESS OF THE SPIRIT.

The witness of the Spirit, according to modern theology, is supposed to supersede every thing else, to give us that full assurance of faith attainable in this life. It is something superadded to faith, by which we are divinely assured of being in a state of grace. This assumes, that faith does not in itself carry with it that divine assurance, which it of course does not, if faith be nothing more than *belief*. Hence what is wanted is not something to be superadded to faith, but *faith* itself; the very thing on which Mercersburg theology insists. What is called the witness of the Spirit, is, after all, according to modern theology, nothing more than something purely subjective, either of an intellectual or emotional nature; for it is simply absurd to speak of the witness of God's Spirit to *our spirits*, when it is denied that we have a *spiritual nature*. By "our spirit," nothing more is meant than our intellectual or emotional nature, and what is called the witness of the Spirit turns out, in most instances, to be nothing more than the natural reaction of that nature from a state of painful distress, into which it had been worked.

According to Mercersburg theology, faith is itself the evidence or authentication of things not seen, and therefore carries within itself that divine assurance. *The Spirit of God speaks* in the Gospel of His Son, and in His sacred ordinances and the official acts of His ministers, *immediately to our spirits*, and the *apprehension* of what God's Spirit witnesses and reveals to our spirits, *that is faith.* The witness of the Spirit is therefore not superadded to faith, but is the revelation of the Spirit of Truth to faith; not simply in reference to our being in a state of grace or our own immediate relation to God, but also in reference to the whole truth of the gospel.

In reference to our immediate relation to Christ, faith has been well defined as the *Christian self-consciousness*, by which we know that we are Christians, with as much certainty as we know that we are human beings by our natural self-consciousness.   That the awakening to a full consciousness of our gracious relation to God in Christ may be sudden, and be accompanied with unspeakable joy in the Holy Ghost, is not only true, but natural, when the transition from unbelief to faith, from darkness to light, is sudden, as was the case in the extraordinary conversion of St. Paul.

CHAPTER VIII.

§ 30.—DOCTRINE OF THE TRINITY.

THE point of difference between modern and Mercersburg theology on this fundamental doctrine of Christianity, does not refer so much to the doctrine itself, as to its relation to faith and the evidence on which its truth is founded; for which reason it here follows, and does not precede the consideration of the nature of faith and evidence.

To establish the doctrine of the Trinity, we must, according to modern theology, rely exclusively on certain passages of Scripture, in which it is implied, or in which divine and distinct personal attributes are ascribed to Father, Son and Holy Ghost. Being incomprehensible to the finite mind, its truth must be accepted on the

bare testimony of the Bible.   Faith in the doctrine of the Trinity is, therefore, nothing more
than an assent of the mind on the strength of
such testimony.   A specious fallacy, which con-
tains but a single truth to redeem it from being
false throughout.   That truth is its acknowledged
mystery.

According to Mercersburg theology, the doctrine of the Trinity is every where presupposed
in the New Testament, as resting primarily on
a divine manifestation or revelation lying back
of the written word, which refers to it but inci-
dentally and impliedly, as existing objective truth
already apprehended as self-evident to faith, and
does not, therefore, labor to prove it, or even to
state it in a direct and formal way.

The Christian idea of the Trinity, like all
other Christian ideas and truths, finds, in the
first place, a basis in the constitution of the
world's life, or in our own nature, which responds
to and apprehends by faith as self-evident, the
revealed fact of the Holy Trinity, as it does that
of the incarnation or any other revealed truth,

which are all alike incomprehensible to the mere understanding.

The doctrine of the Trinity does not rest primarily on any passages of the Bible, from which alone its truth could be established. To find the full and proper evidence of this doctrine, we must go behind the written word, and find it in the self-evidencing *fact* itself, that God has manifested and continues to manifest himself as a Triune Being to the general life of humanity in the great work of the world's redemption, and which ever repeats itself to the consciousness in the experience and life of every individual Christian or subject of that salvation. It is thus as much an object of *faith*, in the *true and proper sense of the word*, and not merely an object of doctrinal *belief*, as any other divine and supernatural reality, the truth of which enters into the Christian consciousness, being apprehended as self-evident by faith.

Modern theology rests on the same false assumption in regard to the Trinity, which it occupies in regard to the Incarnation. Both facts are made to hold a purely outside relation to the world's life and that of individuals, and do not enter into the constitution of that life in a real and living way to work out its salvation. Hence the evidence in favor of the doctrine depends equally on outside testimony alone, on the strength of which mere belief, at best, is attainable. But our baptismal relation to God the Father, Son and Holy Ghost, is in itself sufficient to set aside the false assumption of modern theology on this point. That relation is a solemn guarantee, that God enters into the work of our personal salvation as a Triune Being, and that he will reveal or manifest himself as such to the faith and consciousness of all, in whom the work of salvation is begun and carried forward to its completion.

The relation here referred to corresponds with the original relation and divine image in which man was created. It held in reference to God as a Triune Being, the shadow and type of which still remain amidst the ruin of his fall, in the constitution of his own nature and the divinely appointed natural relations of his earthly life; and when his right relation to God is again restored by the Christian salvation, it will be found to consist in a conscious and proper relation to God the Father, Son and Holy Ghost, each of whom in unity have their peculiar work to do in the world's redemption, as well as in that of individuals.

We accordingly find the manifestation or revelation of God as a Triune Being to the world's life, to fall into three grand world historical periods, answering to the trinity of the world's own proper life. The manifestation of God the Father falls within the period of the world's childhood and youth, in which the parental and filial relation between God and the race becomes manifest. The manifestation of God the Son falls in the central period of the world's history, at the point at which its life had reached its ripened natural manhood. It was then, and not before, that the Son of God himself became Man,—our Brother, and established the fraternal relation between himself and the race. The third and last grand

8

period is that of the manifestation of God the Holy Ghost, by which the new race is brought into living union or marriage relation to God. The Trinity in our natural human life, and in our divinely appointed relations in life—the filial, the fraternal and the marriage relations— finds its true sense and meaning in our three- fold relations to God the Father, who adopts us as his children; to God the Son, who becomes our elder brother; and to God the Holy Ghost, by whom our marriage relation to God is con- summated.   All this enters into the conscious experience of the general, as well as the indivi- dual life of the race as redeemed through the Christian salvation, and hence we must seek in Christianity itself the proper evidence of the doctrine in question, and not in any thing lying outside of it and beyond it.

§ 31.—THE DISTINCT PERSONALITIES.—THE ETERNAL SONSHIP.

Modern theology holds to the distinct person- alities, and that Christ is the natural and eternal

Son of God, having a distinct personality from the Father. The truth of this doctrine, however, can be established only by the teachings of the Bible on evidences lying outside of Christianity, and consequently can challenge simply the assent of our judgment. It is thus left an object of speculation or belief, and not an object of faith, or absolute certainty.

According to Mercersburg theology, the eternal sonship, or the distinct personality of the Son of God, is an object of faith or absolute certainty, as well as any other supernatural reality revealed to man.

With regard to the distinct personality of the Father, there is no question among those who believe in a personal God. He is not only the Father of our Lord Jesus Christ, who is the natural and eternal Son of God, but he is unquestionably also Our Father, by creation and adoption. As such *He* can never become any thing else to us! *He, our Father*, can never become *our Brother.* In order that *God* may become *our Brother*, there must of necessity be a natural and eternal *Son of God*, as a distinct person from the Father.

The truth of the distinct personality of the Son of God, therefore, finds its response in the constitution and necessity of our own nature, which is created for just such a fraternal as well as filial relation; the full sense and meaning of which is not realized, but simply foreshadowed by its relations to the creature in the sphere of our natural life. As a man's natural father is of necessity a distinct person from his brother, so God our Father, and God our Brother cannot be resolved simply into a different manifestation and relation of the *same person*, without involving a figment and a contradiction repugnant to all right feeling implanted in our nature. To come to our right relation to God, as foreshadowed in the constitution of our nature and the life of the world, we must learn to know and to love God, not simply as our Father, but also as our Brother, and not simply as Father and Brother, but enter into that higher and purer joy and love in that still closer and holier relation with God, which is typified by the marriage relation. This *trinity of relations* can only hold with a *trinity of persons* in the divine Being, to meet the demands and wants of our nature. The truth of the distinct personalities thus enters into the Christian consciousness, with the same full assurance of faith, as any other truth is apprehended by faith; amounting not simply to doctrinal belief, but to absolute certainty.

In confirmation of what we have already said, we will yet add, that the whole truth here presented rests ultimately in the *nature of God himself*, as revealed to us in the moral law, which is, at the same time, the law of our own nature, the law of love to God and Man. All the duties required by the law of love to our fellow men are comprehended in the filial, the fraternal and marriage, or parental relation, comprehending, at the same time, the whole of our life, reaching from childhood upwards, until it has itself ripened into parentage, and requiring the totality of all the powers of our being in its full and proper exercise. *Love*, in its first and earliest form, exists as *filial love*, love to the authors of our being, the protectors and pre-servers of our life, who exercise towards us necessarily, justly and rightfully parental authority, and in this relation prepare us for the higher relations and duties of life. Developed in a higher, freer and purer form, it exists as *fraternal love*—love to our fellow beings, with whom we come to stand related as our brothers and equals. As a still higher, purer and holier affection, it is developed in the marriage and parental relation, in which it reaches its highest degree of purity and perfection. But all this, after all, is but typical of something higher, the full sense and meaning of which is realized in our relation and love to God, who of necessity is a Triune Being to be the author of a being constituted like Man, and the Giver of a moral law, such as He has implanted in our nature.

This higher sense and meaning of our natural life is being reached in the *sphere of the Christian life*, which, though a higher order of life, is yet truly human, as well as divine, and therefore corresponding in all respects with the constitution of our proper natural life; and all the duties and privileges of the Christian life are comprehended in corresponding relations, reaching from our *spiritual childhood* upwards, until we become *men* and *fathers in Christ*. In these several relations and stages of its development, our faith and love are evolved and characterized in their several degrees or stages of its progress. Our conscious fellowship is with the Father, and with the Son, and with the Holy Ghost; but first with the Father, then with the Son, and then with the Holy Ghost. Each of these stages of the Christian consciousness—or of our faith and love—is peculiar and distinctive, and they determine the three prominent types of Christianity, as these are found to exist in the actual life of individual Christians, and the life of the Christian Church.

§ 32.—THE TRINITY AND THE CHURCH.

Modern theology admits a certain kind of development of the Christian life, or growth in the grace and knowledge of Christ, but it is in full accordance with its abstract idea of Christianity and the Church, which is at all times and in all ages universally the same. The Church is not the embodiment of Christianity in any real way; and consequently no account is made of its concrete and organic development under any form. The Catholic, the Lutheran and the Reformed Churches, as such, are alike but human organizations, and not truly and really the product of the life of Christianity. They are on a par with any modern sect, that has sprung into existence at the will and dictation of a discontented party, without any historical necessity of any kind.

We have already stated, that the fundamental idea of the constitution of our own nature, corresponds with the fundamental idea of Christianity. That idea is the Trinity, which is fundamental to the whole *Christian life*, no less than to the whole system of *Christian doctrine*. The different manifestations and types of Christianity in the Church, as well as in its individual members, must therefore be reducible to this fundamental idea. The facts in the case, which are patent to every one who will examine them, confirm the correctness of this position. We accordingly find, that as Father, Son, and Holy Ghost are distinct, and yet the one only true and eternal God, so the three great branches of the Christian Church, the Catholic, the Lutheran, and Reformed, are equally distinct and characteristic, and yet constitute the one true Church of God on earth. Each of them is truly and really the legitimate and historical product of the organic life of Christianity; and *the distinctive types of Christianity which they present, bear the impress of that distinction, which has its ultimate and fundamental ground in the Trinity!* The legalistic type of Catholic Christianity finds its prototype in the legalism of the ancient Church, under the dispensation of the Father; the freer evangelical type of Lutheran Christianity finds its prototype in the faith and love of the disciples of Christ, whilst he was objectively present with them on earth, leaning on and trusting

in, as it does, the *objective* Christ—Christ on the
Cross, Christ in the Word, and Christ in the
Sacrament; whilst the Reformed type finds its
prototype in the more spiritual nature of early
Christianity, making proper account of the ope-
rations and witness of the Spirit, or the *subjective* Christ, the Christ within us. In view of
these fundamental characteristics, there is a true
and profound meaning in calling the one the
Church of the Father, the other the Church of
the Son, and the other the Church of the Holy
Ghost, and that these three are one.

§ 33.—THE CHURCH OF THE FUTURE.

That this great fundamental doctrine of Christianity—the Holy Trinity—is underlying the
Christian Church in its actual historical development, and finds in it a most remarkable confirmation, is self-evident to all who will simply
glance at the actual facts in the case. It remains for the *Church of the Future* to realize
their *unity*, as an equally important and neces-

sary historical process, and the guarantee for
that future unity is precisely the great underlying fact of the *presence of God in her ·as a*
TRIUNE BEING, who will present unto himself a
Church without spot and blemish, in which the
Catholic, the Lutheran, and Reformed idea and
type of Christianity will complete each other, in
that higher unity and perfection, which her *tri-
nitarian* life will ultimately work out to completion in a regular process of historical development;—and when the intercessory prayer
of the Saviour will yet be fully realized: "Holy
Father, keep through thine own name those
whom thou hast given me, that they all may be
*one, as thou, Father, art in me, and I in thee,
that they also may be one in us,* that the world
may believe that thou hast sent me;"—and when
the apostolic benediction will enter fully into
the consciousness of all believers: "The grace
of the Lord Jesus Christ, and the love of God
(the Father) and the communion of the Holy
Ghost, be with you all;" and when our undoubted Christian faith will be universally re-

sponded to in a deeper and profounder apprehension of its glorious truths: "I believe in God, the Father Almighty, Maker of heaven and earth, and in Jesus Christ, His only begotten Son, our Lord: who was conceived by the Holy Ghost, born of the Virgin Mary; suffered under Pontius Pilate, was crucified, dead, and buried; He descended into hell; the third day He rose from the dead; He ascended into heaven, and sitteth at the right hand of God the Father Almighty; from thence he shall come to judge the quick and the dead. I believe in the Holy Ghost, the Holy Catholic Church, the communion of saints, the remission of sins, the resurrection of the body, and the life everlasting. Amen."

NOTES.

1. ANTHROPOLOGY.—Locke's empiricism is older than Locke. It is the philosophy of the abstract understanding, underlying the thinking of men in all ages, who elevate and recognize the mere understanding as the judge in matters of faith and religion. Whether men are conscious of the fact, or willing to admit it or not, it is the empiricism as taught, not originated, by the English philosophers, which underlies the thinking, as this meets us every where in modern theology. It meets us more or less clearly, at every point of contrast which we have instituted with that altogether different mode of thinking, which underlies Mercersburg theology, from first to last. It meets us in the fact, that modern theology reverses the order of faith and knowledge; that it admits no premises; that it proceeds without faith in any thing; that it refuses to accept the Creed as a starting-point; that it professes to get its faith fresh from the Bible, &c. If this be not the position of modern theology, then

what is it? What other faith, either objective or subjective, has it, from which it proceeds? What are the admitted premises, or self-evident truths from which it starts? It has none other, and lays claim to none other. It proceeds on Locke's false assumption, that it must and can prove every thing by outside evidence. Whatever has become of Locke's philosophy among philosophers, it is still the underlying principle of the modern theological habit of thought. That Locke has been superseded by other philosophers, either for the worse or the better, decides nothing in regard to the question, What philosophy underlies modern theology? Theology is not reconstructed every decade, to suit itself to every new system of philosophy that starts into existence. Locke's system will never cease to be the controlling principle and habit of modern thinking, as long as the bare understanding is recognized as the umpire in matters of faith and religion.

2. FEDERAL HEADSHIP.—We did not, and do not deny, that modern theology teaches a certain

kind of federal headship of Christ; but it is in
full accordance with its peculiar views of Christianity on other points. It resolves the federal
headship of Christ into a mere abstraction. Apprehending Christ as a mere individual, he becomes the surety in law for a race that stands
outside of him, and to which he stands related
in the constitution of his own person simply as
an individual, and not as its actual source and
fountain. According to Mercersburg theology,
Christ is the federal head of the race by virtue
of what he is in the constitution and law of his
own person, as the actual source and fountain of
the race as redeemed in him. It is only thus
that an actual parallel is established between
the first and the second Adam, and that the one
can take the law place of the other. The attempt to establish a parallel between them, by
resolving the federal headship of the first pro-
genitor of the race into a similar abstraction, is
in contradiction to the fact, that Adam's sin is
imputed to his posterity, because they are actually involved in it, by virtue of their having been

comprehended in his person when he sinned and fell. The idea is a mere figment, that Adam entered into a covenant with a law outside of the constitution of his own person, in order to compromit his posterity in any thing; nor could the justice of the law accept any such arbitrary and abstract arrangement. Adam has not made, and was not capable of making, such a covenant for his posterity. He sinned and fell, and in doing so, he not simply violated the objective law, but the law of his own being, and thus involved his posterity in the ruin of his fall, and its consequences.

3. PARTAKING OF THE HUMANITY OF CHRIST.— It is claimed in favor of modern theology, that it does not repudiate as obsolete the doctrine that believers partake of the humanity of Christ, because it teaches that believers have part in his Spirit. But who does not know, that it so separates the two, as to teach that we can have part in his Spirit, without having part in his humanity? That we cannot have part in his Spirit, without at the same time partaking of his huma-

nity, is what Mercersburg theology, and not what modern theology teaches.

4. JUSTIFICATION.—The attempt is futile to prove, that modern theology agrees with Mercersburg theology in its teaching in regard to justification. As long as it is denied, that we have part in the humanity of Christ, justification on account of his merits is a mere abstraction, an outward imputation, without any participation in them in fact: no difference how men may word their language to express it, by which they only deceive themselves and others. If modern theology teaches that we have part in Christ's humanity, why does it not say so; why not speak it out in plain and unmistakable language? The reason is, because it does not believe, nor teach any thing of the kind.

5. OUR REVIEWER.—The foregoing notes cover the ground so far as a writer in the *Messenger*, whom we take to be Dr. B., thought proper to review our articles. With those notes appended and read in connection with the series, we submit whether any of the Reviewer's excep-

tions are well taken, and whether he was justifiable in displaying his want of courtesy towards us personally. We think, that as a gentleman, he owes us, as well as the Church, an apology, for the spirit and manner which he allowed himself to betray.

We would here take occasion to say, that our object, in writing this treatise, was not to provoke a newspaper controversy. Our object was stated in the introduction; but if any one, who took exceptions to any part of it, when it first appeared in the columns of the *Messenger*, would have been kind enough to point out any actual misrepresentations, we would have been thankful for the correction, because we had contemplated its publication in a more permanent form, and would have been glad to correct any thing that was founded on a misconception of the actual truth which we have endeavored to present. But our Reviewer has failed to convince us that any of his exceptions were well taken; nor do we think that he himself, on reflection, can be of that opinion.

We would, in conclusion, simply remind our Reviewer, that his charges of misrepresentations, &c., if well founded, hold against Dr. Hodge and other champions of modern theology, rather than against us. Get these gentlemen to say, that there is no difference between modern and Mercersburg theology on the points contrasted in our articles! No, they are much too consistent to do any thing of the kind. If they are ever convinced of the truth of Mercersburg theology, which they have been combating, they will not, we trust, set up the claim, that they and their system of theology have been teaching the same thing all along; nor can we see how any minister of our Church will exalt himself in their opinion, *who will forget himself and what is due to his own Church, so far* AS TO DO IT FOR THEM!

Date Due

CPSIA information can be obtained at www.ICGtesting.com
Printed in the USA
LVOW012231140912

298808LV00003B/348/P